Serena Williams

By Adrianna Morganelli

CRABTREE
Publishing Company
www.crabtreebooks.com

CRABTREE
PUBLISHING COMPANY
WWW.CRABTREEBOOKS.COM

Author: Adrianna Morganelli

Editor: Crystal Sikkens

Proofreader: Lorna Notsch

Photo research: Crystal Sikkens, Ken Wright

Design and prepress: Ken Wright

Print coordinator: Katherine Berti

Photo Credits

Alamy: p 16, © Globe Photos/ZUMAPRESS.com; p 19, WENN Ltd; p 21, CTK; p 22, © Globe Photos/ ZUMAPRESS.com; p 24, ZUMA Press, Inc.; p 28, Adam Stoltman/Alamy Live News

AP Images: p 12, FRED JEWELL; p 27, FPS FOR ALLSTATE FOUNDATiON PURP

Everett Collection: p 15, © 20th Century Fox Film Corp.

Getty: p 5, Clive Brunskill; p 7, Mike Pont; p 8, Popperfoto; p 9, Paul Harris; p 10, Ken Levine; p 11, Caryn Levy; p 13, Gary M. Prior; p 17, Chris Polk; p 20, Julian Finney; p 23, John Parra; p 25, Neilson Barnard; p 26, SIMON MAINA / Stringer

Keystone: front cover, Keystone Press via ZUMA Press

Shutterstock: title page, Leonard Zhukovsky; p 14, pdrocha; p 18, DAE Photo;

Wikimedia: p 4, Edwin Martinez

Every effort has been made to trace copyright holders and to obtain their permission for use of copyright material. The authors and publishers would be pleased to rectify any error or omission in future editions. All the Internet addresses given in this book were correct at the time of going to press. The author and publishers regret any inconvenience caused if addresses have changed or sites have ceased to exist, but can accept no responsibility for any such changes.

Library and Archives Canada Cataloguing in Publication

Morganelli, Adrianna, 1979-, author
    Serena Williams / Adrianna Morganelli.

(Superstars!)
Includes index.
Issued in print and electronic formats.
ISBN 978-0-7787-4842-7 (hardcover).--
ISBN 978-0-7787-4871-7 (softcover).--
ISBN 978-1-4271-2098-4 (HTML)

    1. Williams, Serena, 1981- --Juvenile literature. 2. African American women tennis players--Biography--Juvenile literature. 3. Tennis players--United States--Biography--Juvenile literature. I. Title. II. Series: Superstars! (St. Catharines, Ont.)

GV994.W55M67 2018   j796.342092   C2018-900283-2
                                        C2018-900284-0

Library of Congress Cataloging-in-Publication Data

Names: Morganelli, Adrianna, 1979- author.
Title: Serena Williams / Adrianna Morganelli.
Description: New York : Crabtree Publishing Company, [2018] | Series: Superstars! | Includes index.
Identifiers: LCCN 2018005822 (print) | LCCN 2018012430 (ebook) | ISBN 9781427120984 (Electronic) | ISBN 9780778748427 (Hardcover) | ISBN 9780778748717 (Paperback)
Subjects: LCSH: Williams, Serena, 1981---Juvenile literature. | African American women tennis players--Biography--Juvenile literature. | Women tennis players--United States--Biography- -Juvenile literature.
Classification: LCC GV994.W55 (ebook) | LCC GV994.W55 M67 2020 (print) | DDC 796.342092 [B] --dc23
LC record available at https://lccn.loc.gov/2018005822

Crabtree Publishing Company
www.crabtreebooks.com   1-800-387-7650

Printed in the U.S.A./052018/BG20180327

Published in Canada
Crabtree Publishing
616 Welland Ave.
St. Catharines, ON
L2M 5V6

Published in the United States
Crabtree Publishing
PMB 59051
350 Fifth Avenue, 59ᵗʰ Floor
New York, New York 10118

Published in the United Kingdom
Crabtree Publishing
Maritime House
Basin Road North, Hove
BN41 1WR

Published in Australia
Crabtree Publishing
3 Charles Street
Coburg North
VIC 3058

CONTENTS

Words that are defined in the glossary are in
bold type the first time they appear in the text.

Her Serene Highness

Hailed as the best female tennis player ever, American athlete Serena Williams is a powerful force on the courts. Her strength as an athlete and unwavering confidence draw excited crowds to her matches. Many give Serena credit for the growth in the popularity of tennis since her professional debut nearly three decades ago.

Queen of the Courts

Serena is an aggressive tennis player with perfect technique. Her career is beyond impressive. She has earned a whopping 23 **Grand Slam** singles victories, more than any other player on the women's professional tour today. Only former tennis greats Steffi Graf and Martina Navratilova have been ranked longer as the number one player in the world.

Serena's serve, which has been clocked at around 120 miles per hour (193 km/h), is regarded as the fastest-ever in women's tennis history.

Family Dynasty

A fierce passion for tennis runs in Serena's family. Her older sister, Venus, is also a professional tennis player and is equally regarded as one of the greatest players in women's tennis. Serena and Venus have teamed up to win many doubles titles, including three Olympic gold medals in women's doubles. In 2002, the Williams sisters together held the highest world rankings in tennis, with Serena ranked at No. 1 and Venus at No. 2.

Super Serve!

Serena is known for her killer serve. Every serve she tosses into the air looks exactly the same, so her opponents have no idea where she is aiming. By the time she hits the ball, it's too late for an opponent to react.

When Serena and Venus team up in women's doubles tournaments, they are a powerhouse pair. They have won a record 22 titles together.

Early Life

Serena Jameka Williams was born on September 26, 1981, in Saginaw, Michigan. Her father, Richard Williams, had worked as a **sharecropper**, and her mother, Oracene Price, worked as a nurse. Serena and her older sister Venus grew up with three of their older half-sisters. Little did Serena know that, before she and Venus were even born, their father had already planned out their destinies.

Baby of the Family

Serena was the youngest of the sisters, and she made the most of being the baby of the family. The girls shared one bedroom, and Serena would take turns sleeping with a different sister each night in their bunk beds. Her sisters say Serena always wanted to win every family competition. Losing was so frustrating for her that her family usually gave in—even if she didn't really win—just to keep the peace. This obsession for winning would serve Serena well in her future tennis career.

"" She Said It ""

"For all their practice, preparation and confidence, even the best competitors in every sport have a voice of doubt inside them that says they are not good enough. I am lucky that whatever fear I have inside me, my desire to win is always stronger."
—time.com, February 4, 2015

Family Ties ●●●●●

The sisters were all very close growing up. Although tennis would dominate her daily life from a young age, Serena also liked doing things that regular kids did. She liked skateboarding, sewing, playing guitar, and later, surfing. Her goal was always to be a tennis champion, but as a kid, she also thought she'd like to be a veterinarian. Her parents knew athletes usually had short careers, and they wanted the girls to succeed not just on the court, but in life. They raised their children to have faith in God and follow "The Williams Life Triangle." The triangle consisted of three values—commitment, confidence, and courage. Serena's father also taught them about their family's history, which included overcoming racism, **segregation**, and poverty to achieve their dreams.

Serena (right) is shown here with her mother (center) and three sisters Lyndrea, Venus, and Isha (from left).

Their Father's Plan

Before Venus and Serena were born, their father had already decided to train his future children to become tennis stars. While watching TV one evening, he had been shocked to see

a female tennis player win tens of thousands of dollars in a match. Few sports offered female athletes that much prize money. Before Richard could train his children, however, he first had to learn to play tennis himself! He and his wife taught themselves by reading books, watching videos, joining a tennis club, and talking with members of the US Tennis Association.

Richard even wrote a plan outlining the methods he would use to achieve his dream for his children.

The Move to Compton

In 1983, Richard decided to move the family to Compton, California—a city known at the time for gang- and drug-related violence. Their mother objected, but Richard argued that raising their daughters in a tough neighborhood would teach them to stand up for themselves. He pointed to the examples of great champions such as boxer Muhammad Ali and human rights activist Malcolm X.

Life Lessons ●●●●●

Serena and Venus were just three and four years old when their father and mother began to teach them how to play tennis. Training in Compton was difficult at first. Richard had a number of run-ins with gang members selling drugs on the neighborhood tennis court. But he didn't give up. Eventually, he and his daughters were left alone to use the court. Growing up, Venus and Serena's lives revolved around daily tennis practice. The girls were homeschooled so they could practice two hours each day. Their father also wanted them to be mentally tough. Once, he got neighborhood children to taunt and swear at Serena and Venus while they played. He hoped it would teach them to take criticism and prepare for the unexpected.

Serena and Venus pose with their dad on the local court in Compton.

On the Rise

Over the next several years, the two sisters developed their tennis skills together. They both began to play in national tournaments. Venus won every junior tournament she entered and caught the attention of agents and trainers. Serena was not far behind her big sister. She was soon ranked number one among players under the age of 10 by the US Tennis Association. But after a year, Richard pulled his daughters out of the tournaments. He worried that competition was putting too much pressure on them at such a young age. He had also overheard racist comments about his daughters while watching in the stands. Their parents wanted them to focus more on school and just be kids.

At just nine years old, Serena had won 46 matches and lost only three playing in the national junior tournaments.

Professional Debut

When Serena was nine years old, their father moved the family once again. This time, they moved to West Palm Beach, Florida, so the girls could attend the Rick Macci Tennis Academy. After four years, Richard took his daughters out of the Macci Academy and began to coach them on his own once more. At the age of 14, Serena felt that she was ready to play in professional tournaments. She made her career debut in 1995 at the Bell Challenge, in Quebec, Canada. She was too young to qualify for the tournament, so organizers awarded her a wild card entry, which allows a player to play who would not have qualified otherwise. Serena played the match against American Annie Miller, and lost in the first round. Although Serena's professional debut had gotten off to a slow start, it would not be long before the world would see what she had to offer.

Serena and Venus are seen here at the Rick Macci Tennis Academy.

That Winning Feeling

Serena played in several more professional tournaments, gaining experience, but not victories. By 1997, she was ranked 304 in the world. The Ameritech Cup in Chicago would be a turning point. Serena defeated Monica Seles, who was ranked 4, and Mary Pierce, ranked 7. This was an astounding achievement! Serena became the lowest-ranked player ever to defeat two Top 10 opponents. By the end of the year, her rank had soared to 99.

Sixteen-year-old Serena celebrates after defeating Monica Seles in the Ameritech Cup tournament.

Grand Slam ●●●●

The dream of every professional tennis player is to win the Grand Slam. The Grand Slam consists of the four most important tennis events held every year: the Australian Open, the French Open, Wimbledon in the UK, and the US Open. Each event offers the highest prize money, ranking points, and media coverage. In 1998, Serena played in her first Grand Slam, but failed to reach the quarterfinals in any of the tournaments. But what caught the attention of most spectators that year was the first professional tennis match in which the Williams sisters faced off against one another. The result? Serena lost to Venus in the second round of the Australian Open. Serena finished up the year ranked World No. 20 behind Venus, who ranked World No. 5.

Venus stretches to return the ball to Serena during the second round at the Australian Open.

" She Said It "

"I am really proud of Venus. She is a total inspiration….She is my toughest opponent. No one has ever beaten me as much as Venus."
—Interview with BBC, January 27, 2017

Unbeatable Sisters

Venus's star rose first in the tennis world. Being 15 months older than Serena, Venus was taller and stronger than her sister when they started playing professionally. Growing up, Serena always looked up to Venus and wanted to be just like her. She copied everything her sister did, from fashion to ordering the same food at restaurants! She also wanted to be as great a player as Venus. Playing well seemed to come naturally to Venus. Serena had to work harder to perfect her skills.

A Team of Rivals

Millions of people have tuned in to watch whenever Serena and Venus square off against one another. The sisters have played each other 28 times in professional tournaments. They credit their upbringing and their training for not allowing a defeat to affect their close relationship.

" She Said It "

"Family's first, and that's what matters most. We realize that our love goes deeper than the tennis game."
–In *The Champion's Comeback: How Great Athletes Recover, Reflect, and Re-Ignite,* by Jim Afremow

Not Just Tennis ●●

Serena and Venus followed the same path together for a long time. They shared a house in Florida for many years, and both attended the Art Institute of Florida after high school. Serena studied fashion design. Both sisters enjoy learning new languages, and Serena is also interested in acting. She has appeared on episodes of a number of TV shows, including the sitcoms *The Bernie Mac Show* and *My Wife and Kids*, as well as the football drama *The Game*.

The famous sisters also did some voice acting for their cartoon characters on an episode of *The Simpsons*.

Serena Slam

Richard had predicted that Venus would win a Grand Slam tournament first. But Serena beat her to the punch by winning the US Open in 1999. This moved Serena out of her older sister's shadow.

Serena's first Grand Slam win made her the second African-American female tennis player to win a Grand Slam singles tournament.

By 2002, Serena was on fire. Determined to win every Grand Slam tournament, she picked them off one by one. Serena met Venus in the final of the French Open. Defeating her number one ranked sister moved Serena up to number 2. At Wimbledon, the sisters faced off again in the final. Serena won again. This moved Serena to No. 1. The sisters faced off once more at the US Open, ending with another victory for Serena. Only the Australian Open remained. Amazingly, Serena met her sister one more time in the finals in 2003. When Serena won, she became the **reigning champion** of all four Grand Slam tournaments. Her achievement became known as the "Serena Slam."

Tragedy Strikes

Serena achieved her ultimate career goal by the young age of 21, but she only had a short time to enjoy it. Years of playing tennis had put a strain on her body, and Serena underwent knee surgery in 2003. Shortly after, the Williams family suffered a terrible tragedy. Serena's oldest half-sister, Yetunde Price, was killed in a drive-by shooting in Compton at the age of 31. Yetunde worked as a personal assistant for both Serena and Venus, and was also a registered nurse and owned a beauty salon. Her sudden death devastated Serena and the rest of her family, who took Yetunde's three young children into their care. Grief-stricken and suffering from injuries, Serena quickly lost her motivation to play tennis.

Serena poses with Yetunde at an awards ceremony two months before Yetunde's death.

She Said It

"Well, violence has affected our lives personally—we lost our sister…. But I think what people don't realize is how violence really affects not only your family, but your friends, your neighbors…everyone."
—At an event in Washington, DC, called "A Family Affair, Presented by Oath" in 2017

17

Overcoming Obstacles

Being regarded as one of the greatest female athletes of all time comes with its share of obstacles. Serena works hard to live up to that title, but being a winner has taken a toll on her body and also made her a target for criticism. She and her family have had to endure harsh comments and accusations from fans, players, and commentators over the years.

Serena has often been criticized for being "overfit" for a female tennis player. However, when she gained weight after Yetunde's death, critics called her unfit.

Injuries and Health Problems

After her knee surgery in 2003, Serena continued to suffer from more injuries. When her ranking sank to 139, Serena found herself suffering from depression. In 2010, she suffered a serious cut to her foot that led to dangerous blood clots in one lung. She had to undergo immediate surgery and take more time off from tennis to recover. Serena credits her faith as a **Jehovah's Witness**, as well as a life-changing trip to West Africa, for improving her mental health and bringing back her confidence.

Controversy

Serena's father has often been criticized for not following the **conventional** tennis path in coaching his daughters. Some people feel he was too much of a showman, trying to draw attention to them. At the Indian Wells Masters tournament in 2001, an injured Venus pulled out of a semifinal match against Serena. People accused their father of pulling her out deliberately to ensure that Serena would automatically go on to the finals. The next day, the crowd booed Serena and her family during the final and the winner's ceremony. Richard and Venus even heard racial insults. Serena vowed not to play the tournament again and stayed away until 2015.

Lost It!

Serena was fined $10,000 for her outburst against a line judge in 2009. She was also fined $500 for breaking her racket during the game.

19

She's No. 1—Again!

During the 2007 Australian Open, Serena fought her way back to the top. She dedicated the win to her late sister Yetunde. By the end of 2009, Serena was ranked World No. 1 again, had won five Grand Slam tournament titles, and had broken the record for the most prize money earned by a female tennis player in one year.

Retirement—Not!

The cut on her foot and blood clots in her lung kept her away from tennis for 12 months, and her fans began to wonder whether she would retire. Serena was not ready to lay down her tennis racket yet though. She began a rigorous training schedule that got her back into top form. It had been two years since Serena had won a major championship, so when she won at Wimbledon in the summer of 2011 it brought her to tears. She had overcome a "disaster year" and was now back on top. She continued to dominate tennis once again and went on to achieve another Serena Slam in 2015.

23rd Grand Slam ●●●●

In 2017, Serena defeated Venus in the final of the Australian Open. This was the seventh time she had won this tournament, and she recaptured the World No. 1 ranking. But more importantly, Serena made history with this victory. It was her 23rd Grand Slam singles title, moving her ahead of German player Steffi Graf, whose record was 22. Only one other record is left to fall for Serena. Australian Margaret Court holds the all-time record for Grand Slam singles titles: 24. And Serena wants it!

A doubles gold at the 2012 Olympics made the sisters the only tennis players in the world to have won four gold medals.

" She Said It "

"I would really like to take this moment to congratulate Venus; she is an amazing person. There is no way I would be at 23 without her. There is no way I would be at one without her. She is my inspiration. She is the only reason I am standing here today, and the only reason that the Williams sisters exist."
—Serena after winning her 23rd Grand Slam at the 2017 Australian Open

Fierce Fashion

When she's not on the court, Serena can be found sitting in the front row at fashion shows all over the world. She has loved fashion since she was a child. Her mother taught her to sew clothes for her dolls, and she studied fashion design in college. Her knowledge of fashion spurred her on to become an **entrepreneur** and create her own clothing line, Aneres, which is her name spelled backward.

Serena cemented her image as a fashion icon in sports when she wore a black catsuit at the 2002 US Open.

On Point on Court

From the beginning, Serena and Venus wore outfits on the court that challenged the sport's traditional white, stiff tennis dresses. The sisters often appeared in bright fabrics decorated with sequins and lace. They also wore hair accessories, such as colorful beads and even diamond tiaras! In 2004, Serena came to play in a denim skirt and knee-high boots. Sadly, officials did not allow her to wear the boots during her matches.

Signature Collection 🎾

In 2009, Serena launched a collection of jewelry and handbags called Signature Statement. A success on the Home Shopping Network (HSN), Serena's line also caught the attention of the fashion industry at a show during New York Fashion Week. Since its launch, Serena's Signature Statement line has grown to include clothing, and Serena has had two more shows to present her innovative designs.

In Design

In 2004, Serena signed a deal with Nike to create a line called the Serena Williams Collection.

Serena shows off her Signature Statement line during a press conference for the Sony Ericsson Open in 2009.

"" She Said It ""

"My designs are inspired by all women. I want women to know that it's okay to love and embrace who you are…to be unapologetically bold and beautiful in anything you're wearing. Through HSN, my Signature Statement collection is about empowering fans everywhere to connect with this message."
—from www.serenawilliams.com

23

Role Model

As an African-American athlete, Serena has dominated in a sport that was traditionally not racially diverse. She is regarded as a role model to young athletes, as well as an **ambassador** for tennis. Aside from her expertise on the court, many young women admire Serena for her positive body image. She takes this role very seriously and tries to pass on the lessons she has learned in life and motivate young people.

Serena gives tennis lessons to children in Florida.

Tennis Ambassador

Serena's and Venus's numerous victories on the court have influenced many young children to take up tennis. Since the Williams sisters hit the tennis scene, many of these new young athletes are female and African American. Serena has said that she is happy to see that tennis has become more popular, and that she and Venus have made an impact on the sport.

Love Match ●●

Serena has tried to squeeze in time for a personal life over the years. She dated on and off, including rapper and producer Common and actor Jackie Long. But she married her love match Alexis Ohanian in New Orleans in 2017. Alexis is an entrepreneur who cofounded the social news website Reddit. Serena gave birth to daughter Alexis Olympia the same year. Her happiness at becoming a mother was overshadowed by another dangerous blood clot right after Alexis was born. The new mother found recovering from the illness while caring for her newborn overwhelming. Her climb back to full health has been difficult. But Serena has never backed away from a challenge.

Pregnant Serena attends a party at the Metropolitan Museum of Art with her husband Alexis.

❝ She Said It ❞

"It's so much work, and I've given up so much. I don't regret it, but...I'd like her [Alexis Olympia] to have a normal life. I didn't have that."
—whether she would put her daughter in tennis, *Vogue* interview, January 2018

Service On and Off the Court

Serena is passionate about bringing awareness to many causes that are important to her. She has supported many charities, including those for breast cancer, Parkinson's disease, AIDS, and childhood autism. But Serena's main focus is on programs that assist **underprivileged** children.

Serena helped fund the construction of a school in Matooni, Kenya.

The Serena Williams Foundation

The Serena Williams Foundation, founded in 2008, helps children in the US whose families have been affected by violence. Her foundation grants university scholarships to underprivileged students, as well as counseling, housing, food, education, and childcare to those in need.

"She Said It"

"Education is the great equalizer. It is a fundamental human right…an open door to a world of possibilities. I am committed to providing children with the resources they need to realize their potential through a quality education."
—www.tennisworldusa.org, August 7, 2017

UNICEF Ambassador 🎾

Serena became an international goodwill ambassador for UNICEF in 2011. Growing up, her parents encouraged her to excel in school, as well as on the courts. Education is important to her, and she works with UNICEF to provide quality education for children in developing countries. This is made possible with programs such as Schools for Africa and Schools for Asia. Before becoming an ambassador, Serena worked with UNICEF in Ghana on a **vaccination** campaign. She volunteered with healthcare workers to **immunize** children against deadly diseases, and helped distribute mosquito bed nets to prevent the spread of malaria.

Purple Power

In 2017, Serena designed two handbags for the Allstate Foundation's Purple Purse campaign. Bidding on the purses helps raise funds for financial education, job training, and business programs for survivors of **domestic** violence.

Purple Purse program ambassador Serena Williams sports a purple purse she designed.

27

What's Next?

At an age when many athletes begin to think about retirement, Serena has returned to play. Defeated in her first match after her return, she realizes she has a lot of catching up to do. But she is determined to reclaim her throne. She still has her sights set on beating Margaret Court's all-time record of 24 Grand Slam singles titles. Serena is well prepared for life beyond the tennis courts, too. Retiring from tennis will leave her more time to conquer the business world, pursue more acting jobs, and enjoy—maybe even expand—her young family. Serena Williams has the world at her feet.

"" She Said It ""

"If you'd asked me 10 years ago where I'd be in 10 years, I would have said I'm going to be retired and have a family. Ten years from now? Hopefully I will have more kids. I would like to sit on another board or two…and promote diversity, both ethnic and sex diversity, and hopefully break down barriers for lots of people."

—www.tennisworldusa.org, August 7, 2017

Timeline

1981: Serena Jameka Williams is born in Saginaw, Michigan, on September 26

1991: The Williams family move to Florida

1995: Serena turns professional, losing her debut tennis match at the Bell Challenge in Quebec, Canada

1998: Serena plays in the Australian Open, her first Grand Slam tournament. She loses to Venus in the second round, 6–7, 1–6.

1999: Enrolls at the Art Institute of Fort Lauderdale in Florida for fashion design

1999: Wins the US Open, becoming the first Williams sister to win a Grand Slam tournament

2002: Ranked World No. 1 for the first time in her career

2002–2003: Completes her first "Serena Slam" by winning all four Grand Slam titles

2003: Has surgery to repair her left knee

2003: Her older half-sister, Yetunde Price, is murdered in Compton, California

2004: Launches Aneres clothing line.

2008: Establishes the Serena Williams Foundation

2009: Launches her jewelry and handbag collection Signature Statement

2010: Has surgery to repair her right foot, after it was cut by stepping on glass

2011: Undergoes emergency treatment for a blood clot in her lungs

2011: Appointed a UNICEF international goodwill ambassador

2016: Wins the Wimbledon title for the seventh time, making it her 22nd victory in a major tournament

2016: Ties Steffi Graf's record for longest consecutive weeks ranked number one

2017: Beats Venus in the Australian Open final, winning her 23rd Grand Slam, surpassing Steffi Graf

2017: Gives birth to a baby girl, Alexis Olympia Ohanian Jr., then undergoes surgery for more blood clots in her lungs

2017: Marries Reddit co-founder Alexis Ohanian

Glossary

ambassador A person who acts as a representative or promoter of a specific activity or cause

conventional Conforming to what is generally done or believed

domestic Relating to the home, household affairs, or family

entrepreneur A person who starts and runs a business, often with great financial risk

Grand Slam The four major tennis tournaments on the international circuit, including Wimbledon, French Open, US Open, and Australian Open

immunize Protect a person or animal from an infection or disease

Jehovah's Witness A member of a religious group that practices a form of Christianity

reigning champion The most recent winner of a competition

segregation A policy that keeps people of different races or religions separate from each other

sharecropper A tenant farmer who gives a share, or part, of the crop to the landlord as rent

underprivileged Being deprived of the same standard of living or rights as most people in a society because of low economic or social status

vaccination Treatment with a substance that protects the body from harmful diseases

Find Out More

Books

Fishman, Jon. M. *Serena Williams.* Amazing Athletes, Lerner Publications, 2016.

Nagelhout, Ryan. *Serena Williams.* Gareth Stevens Publishing, 2016.

Ransome-Cline, Lesa. *Game Changers: The Story of Venus and Serena Williams.* Simon & Schuster Canada, 2018.

Websites

Serena Williams's official website
www.serenawilliams.com

Instagram photos and videos of Serena Williams
www.instagram.com/SerenaWilliams

Index

About the Author

Adrianna Morganelli holds degrees in English language and literature and fine arts and has a diploma in professional writing. Her professional career includes working as an editor for Crabtree Publishing and authoring many nonfiction books for children. Adrianna is currently a freelance writer and editor, and also writes children's fiction chapter books.